HOW TO ANALYZE PEOPLE

----- ≈≈≈≈≈ -----

Get to know what people are thinking and respond in the best possible way - gain distinct advantage in social, personal, and professional environments

Wallace Foulds

Text Copyright © 2018 Wallace Foulds

All rights reserved. No part of this guide may be reproduced in any form without permission in writing from the publisher except in the case of brief quotations embodied in critical articles or reviews.

Legal & Disclaimer

The information contained in this book is not designed to replace or take the place of any form of medicine or professional medical advice. The information in this book has been provided for educational and entertainment purposes only.

The information contained in this book has been compiled from sources deemed reliable, and it is accurate to the best of the Author's knowledge; however, the Author cannot guarantee its accuracy and validity and cannot be held liable for any errors or omissions. Changes are periodically made to this book. You must consult your doctor or get professional medical advice before using any of the suggested remedies, techniques, or information in this book.

Upon using the information contained in this book, you agree to hold harmless the Author from and against any damages, costs, and expenses, including any legal fees potentially resulting from the application of any of the information provided by this guide. This disclaimer applies to any damages or injury caused by the use and application, whether directly or indirectly, of any advice or information presented, whether for breach of contract, tort, negligence, personal injury, criminal intent, or under any other cause of action.

You agree to accept all risks of using the information presented in this book. You need to consult a professional medical practitioner in order to ensure you are both able and healthy enough to participate in this program.

TABLE OF CONTENTS

FOREWORD 1

AN INTRODUCTION TO ANALYSIS 3

CHAPTER 1–IN THE BEGINNING 7
   Why Should I Analyze? 11

CHAPTER 2 –BODY LANGUAGE: UNDERSTANDING NONVERBAL COMMUNICATION 19
   How to Read Body Language? 21
   The Most Common Body Language Patterns 28

CHAPTER 3 – READ 'EM, SENSE EMOTIONAL ENERGY, TRUST YOUR INSTINCT 35
   How Do I Start Reading People? 37
   How Do I Use My Instinct to Analyze People? 41

CHAPTER 4 - UNDERSTANDING HUMAN PERSONALITY TYPES - DISC MODEL OF HUMAN BEHAVIOR 51
   Origins of the DISC model 52
   The Fundamentals of the DISC Model 53
   Things to Remember Before you Begin Defining Personality Traits 56

DEFINING PERSONALITY TRAITS 58

SOME FURTHER TIPS 64

CHAPTER 5 – GETTING THE BEST OUT OF EVERY CONVERSATION 67

CONCLUSION 81

FOREWORD

This book is a one-stop source of information on reading the nonverbal aspects of human interaction. As any seasoned psychologist will tell you, verbal communication is only a small part of how we communicate with others. All our actions have a certain impact on others and vice versa. Knowing, recognizing and understanding the underlying cause of these can be of immense help for everyone.

In this ebook, we have attempted to bring together profound knowledge on human behavior combined with in-depth analysis of its causes and concerns. We show how seemingly unrelated actions or gestures are in fact part of a synchronous whole and when viewed from a larger perspective, give deep and revealing insights into people and their personalities. It is our sincere wish to add to the blossoming understanding of human interactions in all contexts of life and foster greater compassion through gnosis or knowing.

Do you want to be a master analyzer with the ability to figure people out right from the time you meet them? This book can give you all the necessary tools of the trade as well as numerous tips and tricks to help you understand people better and analyze their personalities in depth.

For the purpose of explaining all aspects of people analyzing, the book has been divided into four broad categories – novice, intermediate, expert and master. As you progress through each chapter, you are advised to go through the contents again and again until you have them committed to memory.

As we humans evolve our ability to communicate with one another, understanding the voluntary and involuntary ways of communication becomes vital. Only by doing this can we strive for greater understanding of our internal and external selves and truly become the mindful and compassionate species so vigorously endorsed by all religions of the world.

AN INTRODUCTION TO ANALYSIS

Pundits are used to analyze the gap between what our ideals suggest and what our security interests require.

---- *Elliott Abrams, Political Scientist*

What did you first feel when you saw this book's title? Curiosity, right?

So did the thousands who have also picked it up. Curiosity is one of our most inherent traits. It's a gift from our genes which continuously compels us to explore the unexplored, scale the uncharted and master the unknown.

So why shouldn't this include exploring and mastering our own lives?

Aren't you curious to know what your spouse is thinking during their 'moods'?

Wouldn't it ease your own anxiety a little to have some insight into their state of mind?

HOW TO ANALYZE PEOPLE

Yes, it would!

In the professional domain, wouldn't it be helpful to know exactly what your boss wants? Or if you are the boss, then wouldn't it be helpful to know how to best place your human resource assets to achieve the next goals? This knowledge is indispensable.

Knowledge is power and thus, our greatest quest. Who doesn't want to be like a Jedi Master with the ability to read people's intentions and influence them? While you might not be able to use "The Force" as explicitly as in the movies, the most successful entrepreneurs and motivators are able to use this ability to greatly enhance a worker's or client's potential.

Whether at home, work or in any social situation, the ability to read people is a great asset and can mean the difference between harmony and discord. You may have often found wives, including your own if you have one, complaining that their husbands just don't get them.

Well, you are not the only one. Many men and women with moody partners have periodically been befuddled by this phenomenon. Also, do you sincerely want to know why your teenager is acting out and what you can do about it?

AN INTRODUCTION TO ANALYSIS

How about that colleague who seems to be the friendliest guy at one turn and a literal sociopath at another? In all of these situations and many more just like them, the ability to read people is an amazing asset.

What you must practice is being mindful, observant and free of any prejudice. It is the only way to truly grasp the essence of things and read what lies between the said and the unsaid. So first, as that famous quote by Bruce Lee goes, you must empty your cup.

In other words, forget what you know or you think you know. Forget the past, forget the future. Be here and now, reading this book and absorbing the wealth of knowledge on analyzing people it offers.

Let the wisdom of centuries of thinkers, philosophers, sociologists, psychologists and even everyday people, guide you towards the most comprehensive take on how to analyze yourself and others.

Through diligent practice and the right guidance, you will be able to cultivate a masterful ability to analyze people and situations. Do note that the results will depend upon how intensely you practice the art and not by how much you have read about it.

HOW TO ANALYZE PEOPLE

There is no substitute for experience and so implementing the ways of analyzing people suggested in this book will go a long way in ensuring you gain the maximum benefit from reading the book.

With that said, you must also be mindfully ethical in your analytical ability. Do not use it to hurt anyone or to give yourself an undue advantage over others, because harm to others inevitably leads to self-harm.

If you keep these things in mind, then with the help of this book, you can become an able analyzer of people and gain insights into their personalities that others can only dream of having.

Want to be a mind reader with everyone's throbbing nerve at your fingertips? Then read on!

CHAPTER 1–IN the BEGINNING

To learn means by practice, by inquiring, by analyzing to find out what is, not what was.

--------- Lobsang Tenzin, Ex-Tibetan Prime Minister

The first step towards analyzing people begins with analyzing yourself. You might have heard the old Latin quote – '*Vincit Qi Se Vincit.*' It means he or she conquers who conquers him or herself.

So why is this quote being mentioned here? It's simple! This quote contains the wisdom of generations of Romans who watched the rise and fall of a great empire. Distilled from their experience, it is an insight into human nature and gives you a gigabyte worth in a nanosecond.

The problem with modern life is that there are so many distractions that people tend to lose focus in a matter of seconds. Some of you might even think that quoting Latin is a sure sign that this stuff is not meant for you, right? Wrong!

HOW TO ANALYZE PEOPLE

There is a reason why people say Old is Gold and it rings true at every turn.

Having said that, conquering your own self is not that easy. Everyone knows that passions rule. And why shouldn't they? Would you pass on this garden of earthly delights for the sake of some supposed insight and forethought? Most people wouldn't. But you are not most people. The fact that you picked this book up and are still reading it proves that you are a bit different.

Back to conquering yourself. Being able to understand your own desires and drives is the first step towards this. Your intentions are the most important thing when trying to understand yourself. The trick is to lead your feelings and emotions and not be led by them.

So, with that in mind, here are some of the biggest things you must consider when trying to figure out yourself and everyone around you:

1. **The Word is Primal**

    Did you know that you actually have two brains? That's right! One's in your skull and the other one is in your gut. It is where all your natural instinct comes from. In tense situations or when you are stressed out, your instinct is

CHAPTER 1—IN the BEGINNING

what you rely on the most. Why do some people say they get butterflies in their stomach when they see a certain person? It's because their instinct is giving them signals that they can't ignore.

So, if you begin acting according to your instinct, you will see results faster than if you were to deny them. Be warned, however. Acting on instinct does not mean acting on impulse. In fact, it means the exact opposite. When you act on impulse, you just do what was most immediate to you and your needs. When you act on instinct, there has been some cognition that has taken place subconsciously and your conscious mind heeds the suggestion.

2. **Feel the Vibe, Ride the Tide**

In the modern world, people are getting more and more disconnected from each other and their immediate surroundings. For example, someone can simply plug in their earphones and completely tune out of the world around them. You must understand that the reason why people are choosing to disconnect is that they don't find fulfillment in the immediate moment.

To counter it, you have to be the opposite. Learn to read the signs any person gives off. Feel their vibe and react accordingly. Everything that happens has a reason. It is up to you to find the cause and act accordingly.

Have you heard the famous line by Bruce Lee – Be water, my friend?

That is exactly what you must be! Water takes the shape of whatever it is poured into. If it meets an obstacle, like a boulder, it just flows around it.

How about that Bear Grylls meme – Improvise, Adapt, Overcome? That is the essence of being and becoming your best self.

3. Inside Out

Since the beginning of human civilization, people have had to channel their drives in line with those of the society which they are a part of. Don't you wish everyone would be more open to your way of thinking? That would be very helpful, right? In every aspect of life, cooperation and coordination is a shortcut to success.

That is why happy families are so content. That is why extroverts are socially capable. That is also why

CHAPTER 1–IN the BEGINNING

businesses which foster a great work culture get the most out of their employees. So, unless you want to be a recluse who lives in the Himalayas, you should learn to work with others. And the best way of doing that? Analyze and understand people!

Why Should I Analyze?

Have you ever had a friend who is just great at handling every situation? They can instinctively grasp the feel of every moment and they always seem to be in control. If you could find out how they work, there's a big chance that you will find they are analyzers. They instinctively read people and situations and make them work to their benefit. Wouldn't it be great if you could do the same? That would be fabulous, right?

You might be thinking that analyzing is hard work and often not worth the effort. Yes, analysis can be mentally taxing. But should that stop you from being able to do it? No! The simple fact is that analyzers enjoy distinct advantages over other people. Want to know what they are? Here's the list:

1. **Analysis Leads to Better Relationships**

    People who analyze themselves and others are always a step ahead of everyone else. Not only do they know more about themselves than most, but they also know more about other people. Being able to intuitively grasp everyone's feelings and emotions is a wonderful asset. However, unless you are born with it, you will need to develop this ability.

We often find we misunderstand or misinterpret people and situations. This leads to discord and relationship problems. Wouldn't you like to have some way to comfort your spouse and assure them of your support? Wouldn't it be perfect if you could tell your business partner that you can weather the decline together? How about Mary, who just went through a terrible divorce and needs support, but is just too self-conscious to ask for it? As a friend, wouldn't you like to be there for her?

In all such situations and virtually every other scenario in life, if you are able to analyze and assess what is required in a situation, then you will most likely be able to take the necessary steps. Adequate analysis can literally pave the way for the best kind of relationships. Right from the start of an acquaintance, if you analyze the other person, then you will have a good idea about them and figure out how reliable they are.

CHAPTER 1–IN the BEGINNING

Trust is a big thing for us all and being able to trust the people around you, whether at home or at work or just in plain-old friendships, can be the difference between being stressed out and being stress-free. Naturally, the more you understand another person, the better your chemistry will be.

2. Analysis Breeds Compassion

Many people think that people who analyze a lot are like machines. They have little emotion and no feelings to speak of. This is a completely mistaken idea. Though analysis does require some amount of emotional disinvestment, once you factor in the value of a person in your life, the benefits are obvious.

As a matter of fact, people who analyze tend to be highly empathetic and caring. Wouldn't it be great if instead of turning your partner off with your standard and clichéd approach, you could understand what they need immediately?

The biggest benefit of analyzing things is that you become more and more aware of other people's inner worth and their place in your life. When you see something from another person's perspective, it naturally produces compassion and clarity. Suppose your sister, who is always a top-level student, suddenly has a drop in grades because of some reason she is not telling anyone. As her sibling, does it not feel natural to try relate to her problems? If you show her that you share a bond, then you can probably find out what is troubling her.

Compassion is key to having good people in your life. If you analyze them and take care of their emotional needs, they will want and value your attention and affection. If you see things from a different perspective, it will naturally foster your own maturity. So, you should make a habit of analyzing the people around you every single day.

3. Analyzers are Self-Content

Analysis is inherent to understanding yourself. When you understand what you need, you don't go chasing the approval of others. You don't do things just because they are trendy or popular. Fads fade sooner than later, and analyzers know better than to seek validation from trying to fit in with passing trends.

CHAPTER 1–IN the BEGINNING

A lot of people do things unthinkingly. Analyzers do the exact opposite. They think things through and are flexible enough to meet the needs of any situation. That is why when the latest trend comes up, they figure out if it works for them. They don't just run with it because it's popular. So, while they might not appear to be very fashionable at the start, they do pack their own sense of style that conforms to their personality.

Wouldn't you like to be a trendsetter instead of a trend follower? Does it not make more sense to act according to your likes and dislikes than simply doing what is 'in' right now? Being an analyzer can give you the tools to craft your own unique personality and become an individual. In a world full of people willing to be led, this is a great attribute to have and should be cultivated regularly.

4. Analysis Breeds Intelligence

Analysis is a mental activity. As thinking is naturally part of our everyday functions, a conscious effort to analyze leads to drastic improvement in intelligence levels. You will find that the most intelligent people you meet are habitual analyzers. In fact, they have been doing it for so long that has become second nature to them.

Do you think the ability to analyze effectively will help you improve on a personal, social and professional level? Do you want to be a trailblazer in your own right? Then analysis and the ability to gauge people, situations, trends and other things in your life are essential to your success. The simple fact is that analysis is a dissection of the human experience. It's like being a neurosurgeon who has hundreds of successful surgeries behind you. The more you practice it, the better you become at it.

5. **Analyzers Help People Grow**

Every analyzer becomes an example for others to follow. They become models of what people should be like and how they should move through their lives. If you want to be someone who can lead, inspire and help others evolve their potential, then analysis is your biggest asset in this regard.

Do you want to help your children grow up to be an individual? Do you want them to be self-reliant, self-sufficient and capable of leading successful, meaningful lives? Then you need to teach them the fine art of analysis. From an early age, children follow whatever their parents do. So in order to bring out their best, you

CHAPTER 1–IN the BEGINNING

need to bring out the best in yourself. And the simplest way to that? Analysis!

So, now you know some of the many benefits that analyzers naturally enjoy. Do you think you have it in you to become a great analyzer? Even if you aren't sure you do, know that there are definite ways that you can develop this ability. Winning is a habit and it starts with the first step. Read the following chapter to know the basics of behavior and body language analysis and get going on becoming an able analyzer.

CHAPTER 2 – BODY LANGUAGE: UNDERSTANDING NONVERBAL COMMUNICATION

Before you get into the mind, you have to inhabit the physicality. Body language is a great way of speaking.

---------- Michelle Yeoh, Actor

Your body is an expression machine. Right from the time we are born, we start expressing how we feel inside by projecting it outwards with our bodies. That is how mothers are able to guess if their infants are doing well or not. That is also how the ablest analyzers are able to gauge a person and their range of emotion.

What does your own behavior say about yourself? Did you know that you could voluntarily or involuntarily be giving signals to the people around you? For example, crossing your arms across your chest may imply that you are feeling impatient or guarded. You will find that many client service industries like hospitality, food service, counseling etc. lay a lot of emphasis on body language and posturing.

If you want to be an analyzer, you must first analyze yourself. Understand what you are giving off to the people around you. Figure out the reasons behind your body language and how to control it

If you are already analyzing people and situations regularly, you may know that there are times when people tend to get tunnel-visioned. For example, you might think that shuffling the feet a lot means that a person is feeling impatient. In reality, it might just mean that they need to go to the bathroom or that they are having trouble with their footwear.

Knowing when and how to interpret things is very important for the correct analysis. As you start, you will sometimes find out that you were wrong. Accept these corrections and take them in your stride. Do not get bogged down by incorrect assumptions. Instead, incorporate the people's different types of body languages and add them to your mental encyclopedia.

With that in mind, let's look at what this chapter will talk about. You will be walked through detailed insights into body language types and behavioral variations. An extensive list of the most common and recurring body language types will be examined

CHAPTER 2 – BODY LANGUAGE: UNDERSTANDING NONVERBAL COMMUNICATION

and evaluated. Want to know how to read people and their actions? Then this is the place to start.

How to Read Body Language?

Have you ever been on a date when the girl is constantly playing with her hair? This might mean that she likes you. How about if your girlfriend/boyfriend constantly checks their phone whilst talking to you? This might mean that they are not particularly interested in the conversation and you need to up the ante a bit.

The first and most important thing to understand when reading body language is that it differs with each person. So you cannot have a standard body language pattern that applies to all. But as you go through with your analyses, you will definitely be able to figure out a commonality in most body languages. There is no one-size-fits-all though. Only you can figure out what each bit of body language means in each unique situation and how it relates to the people you meet during your days and nights.

A very important factor when considering body language is the culture. We are all, to a certain degree, the product of our cultural conditioning. Knowing what the culture prescribes and what it doesn't can narrow down your speculative range when it comes to reading emotions.

For example, Americans tend to have a considerably different style of body language from Chinese people. They tend to be more expressive and physically affectionate. Also, some cultures see eye contact as a sign of paying attention, while others see it as a sign of disrespect.

So, before you draw conclusions, consider culture and the setting. Also, be sure not to analyze one piece of body language in isolation. You need to take several aspects of a person's body language and consider what they mean together as a whole...

With that out of the way, let's dive into the some of the most common body language and behavioral types commonly seen today:

1. **It's All in the Eyes**

    Shakespeare once wrote, "The Eyes are the windows to your soul." Nearly 500 years later, his words still ring true! Have you ever been fascinated with someone's eyes? It happens a lot to people who love openly. There is a certain mystique about them that cannot be denied.

    Whether a person is lying or not, the eyes seldom lie. Make a habit of looking into people's eyes. This will make you appear confident and attentive and also enable you

CHAPTER 2 – BODY LANGUAGE: UNDERSTANDING NONVERBAL COMMUNICATION

to spot emotional changes in the person you are observing.

For example, the pupils dilate with certain mental activities. If someone is lying, then they will may avert eye contact, look downward or elsewhere. On the other hand, if someone is lying, they may stare too hard at you. If you are on a date and your date is not looking at you directly, then this might mean they are feeling pressured or guarded. It would be smart to make them feel at ease and let them open up to you.

Similarly, if your employee keeps looking elsewhere during the meeting or presentation, it could mean they are not interested. If you are the employee, make sure you maintain a constant, yet humble eye contact with your boss or immediate superior.

2. **Poker Face**

Do you ever wonder why people like to lay so much emphasis on their facial features? Why women and even some men spend time sculpting their faces to perfection? It is because the face is the roadmap to anyone's personality. The fact that everyone other than the person themselves can see and observe the face means that we are especially cautious of what we reveal from our facial expressions.

Learn to read the face and its expression and you have a pretty good idea of what the person is feeling. You are highly likely to get a lot of visual cues into the person and their thought process. The most common facial expression is the smile. Broadly speaking, there are three types of smiles – genuine, fake and the often hard-to-understand, half-smile.

Genuine smiles take up the whole face. Every part of the face, especially the eyes, will be involved and in many cases, the face will be accompanied by a glow. The fake smile will only involve the mouth and will be short-lived. The half-smile usually takes up only part of the face and is indicative of sarcasm. Besides these, if a person feels forced to play act, then they will most likely adopt a grimaced smile.

Some people are really good at hiding their true intentions and feelings. While it might be hard to read them, it is possible if you observe very closely. Not even the most deceptive sociopaths are able to live with grace and complete conviction.

CHAPTER 2 – BODY LANGUAGE: UNDERSTANDING NONVERBAL COMMUNICATION

3. Hand-made

Have you ever met a person who used their hands a lot to express themselves? Did they have quite visible body movements to express their inner feelings too? Then that person will probably have a pretty robust self-expression mechanism. A lot of people use their hands to express or make gestures to support and augment their vocalizations.

Sometimes people use their hands to emphasize that what they are saying is important. You can do the same and it is more likely to keep your listener's attention on you. This is especially useful when addressing a group of people, whether at work or anywhere socially.

Have a look at how politicians or pastors address their congregations. Don't they seem like they are conducting a symphony? Controlling the ebb and flow of the audience's emotions through their words and hand gestures? This is a highly coveted oratorical quality. If you plan to be a promising entrepreneur, then this ability is vital for your leadership skills.

You can gauge the leadership ability of a person through these physical gestures and actions. Be mindful of how they use their gestures and how they relate to their words and their voice. Once you start understanding how to interpret them effectively, you should have no trouble sifting between the genuine and the fake.

4. Focus on the Feet

Ever wondered why some people are constantly shuffling their feet or shifting from one stance to another? This is one of the more ignored nonverbal aspects of communication. Most people are so focused on controlling their facial and upper body expressions that they completely forget the lower-half and all that they are suppressing or holding back comes out through their feet.

So for example, if someone is having a conversation with you, but their feet are not pointed in your direction, that means they want to be wherever their feet are pointing. Also, if a person has a slouched posture or slightly bent at the knees, then they could possibly not be interested in the conversation. Another strong indicator may be if they are moving from one position to another. This can be indicative of them being preoccupied with something else.

CHAPTER 2 – BODY LANGUAGE: UNDERSTANDING NONVERBAL COMMUNICATION

When it comes to ladies, the way they hold their feet and their posture is a big cue. You will find that most sophisticated women stand with their right knee slight bend inward. This is considered a sign of their femininity. Be wary, however, that just because a woman stands in some other way, it does not make her any less of a woman.

5. **Proximity Alert!**

Have you ever found that getting close to someone can be very sensually or emotionally satisfying? You are not the only one! We naturally tend to want to be closer to the people we feel connected with. This differs from person to person and setting to setting.

For example, your potential boyfriend might get tentatively close to you to exhibit his interest. But your boss might get close to you to reinforce his or her dominance. Similarly, children always want their mothers to be in close proximity. When they are not, the children are likely to feel insecure.

This need for close proximity is symbolic of our sociability. A good sign in any budding romantic relationship is the comfort of being close together. At work, you might get partnered with a person and depending upon the chemistry between the two of you, your performances will differ.

If you want to control your expression of interest, this is a rule of thumb you can follow. Test the waters first. See how comfortable a person is with you being close and far. Let your instinct guide you as to when to move closer or go far. Once you have a handle on their proximity margins, you can play it as you wish. Be mindful of the situation and the minute changes in their reactions to your proximity to them.

So, that covers the fundamentals of body language. Remember to keep your entire visual acuity on the person(s) you are speaking to and let your analysis run in the background. Once you have developed the habit, it should come naturally and all indicators will automatically get registered in your mind.

Now, let us move on to the macro–behavioral analysis.

The Most Common Body Language Patterns

Wouldn't you like to instantly get to know and understand a person you just met? In all spheres of life, doesn't that make your job a lot easier? Indeed it does! Body language analysis is

CHAPTER 2 – BODY LANGUAGE: UNDERSTANDING NONVERBAL COMMUNICATION

at the core of understanding a person and their personality. It is literally taking a peek under someone's skin and figuring out what makes them tick.

Body language is linked to behavior and how people project themselves in society. That is why the people you see every day are more likely to know you better than any random stranger. That is because you have revealed yourself to their eyes over time. However, an attentive and observant analyzer will be able to get a fair idea of your personality within just a few interactions. Here are some of the most important body language patterns to watch for:

1. **Avoiding Eye Contact**

   Does your child always try to avoid making eye contact with others? Then chances are they are hiding something from you. Does your employee do the same? Then they might be hiding something too or just feeling less-than-confident around you. It would be wise to address the problem quickly in both cases.

2. **Pupil Dilation**

   If you are a keen observer, then you might be able to notice how a person is feeling by the dilation of their pupils. For example, when on a date, if the guy/girl has dilated pupils, then they might be enjoying themselves. On the other hand, if their pupils have contracted, then you just said something they didn't like and you should remedy the situation fast.

3. **They are Always Smiling**

Have you ever met someone like that? Some people have a perpetual smile on their face at all times. Does it not seem slightly strange? Most people would say it does. In fact, if someone is smiling all the time, then that means that they are either faking or hiding their true feelings. It is relatively easy to spot a real smile from a fake one. A real one will light up the whole face, while a fake one will involve only the lips.

4. **Skin Coloring**

Along with smiling, blushing is one of the major giveaways that the person is into you or feeling something intimately. On a date, watch out for these signs. At work, you can take note of how your coworkers and subordinates look. If they have dark lines under their eyes, they might be feeling tired. If they color up when you joke with them, chances are that you touched the right chord.

CHAPTER 2 – BODY LANGUAGE: UNDERSTANDING NONVERBAL COMMUNICATION

5. Tone of Voice

The tone of voice is one of the best indicators of how a person is feeling at the moment. Have you ever been to McDonald's where an employee had a particularly bland tone of voice? This is a sign that they do not enjoy their job or are overworked and tired. At home, always be mindful of the tone of voice of your spouse, children and other loved ones. Let your instinct guide you in understanding their frame of mind. If they seem excessively chatty or unusually detached, then you must react accordingly.

6. They Cross Their Arms Across the Chest

Do you ever involuntarily do this one? If so, then you should be mindful not to. Crossing your arms across your chest is indicative of being vulnerable, reserved, defensive or unwilling to engage. There are some situations that can make you feel like that, but you should avoid acting this way. On the other hand, if you see someone doing this action, then it is best to back off and let them open up to you instead of prodding them to reveal themselves.

7. They Put Their Hands in Their Pockets

Hands in the pockets are a good thing for casual settings. But does it seem alright in a work environment? No. Never do that at work, even with coworkers. Even if it is cold, try to avoid this habit because it is a sign that you are not particularly enthusiastic about what's going on. If you work in the hospitality industry, always hold your hands together in front of you pointing downwards or by the sides of your body. Even in corporate environments, it is best to maintain an active and engaged body language.

8. They Shift Their Posture a Lot

This one is a sure sign that the person is feeling uncomfortable. Shifting your weight from one leg to another or changing your hand positions quickly indicates that you are feeling restless and would like to be elsewhere. Have you ever come across a person like that? If you find someone behaving such then you might want to put them at ease by having some relaxing conversations.

Over and above all the ones that we have mentioned here, there might be many other body language indicators that differ by

CHAPTER 2 – BODY LANGUAGE: UNDERSTANDING NONVERBAL COMMUNICATION

personality and situations. Remember that you must always analyze body language according to the circumstance.

For example, if you are being questioned by the police, shifting around is quite natural. But if your date shifts around a lot, it may be a sign that he or she is not into you.

When you start interpreting body language, you might be wrong often, but do not give up. Just learn from your mistakes and sooner rather than later, you will be able to gauge people correctly.

The next chapter is going to be all about harnessing your instinct to help you to read people. However, it is recommended that you first understand the basics underlined in this chapter thoroughly before moving on to the next one.

For those of you who feel confident that they have already done that, the question is – are you ready to become an analysis machine by instinct? If so, then read on to learn how to habituate your instinct into an analytical marvel!

CHAPTER 3 – READ 'EM, SENSE EMOTIONAL ENERGY, TRUST YOUR INSTINCT

"True deduction can only be obtained through a certain amount of self-annihilation."

— Joe Riggs

Did you get what that quote above means? It means that before you even begin to analyze someone, you must divest yourself of any prejudices you might have. Don't you wish sometimes that you had not misunderstood that jock-looking guy's intentions? He might have actually been a great boyfriend. Now he belongs to one of your friends. How about that nerdy girl in class you thought was weird? She turned out to be quite the babe now. If only you had not been so quick to judge her, you could've hit something off.

It's a very common misconception that people only behave according to certain established stereotypes. These clichés do exist for a reason, but you will always be able to find people who don't conform to any of the usual personalities that you can read in a psychology textbook. This is where you have to get creative. The ability to spot different influences and indicators in anyone's personality is of vital importance for figuring them out. You need to mix and match the different aspects of any given individual's personality and understand where they stand.

The depth at which analyzing people will be discussed in this chapter is at least at the intermediate level. So, if you feel you still have to get a good hold over the fundamentals, you should go and read the previous chapter again. That is the foundation of your thinking and analytical ability when it comes to people. So, the clearer you are on the basics, the better your chances of understanding this chapter will be.

For those of you who think they already understand all that, this chapter will explain what you need to do to become an intermediate-level people analyzer. It will give you the tools to carry out your own analyzes of people and develop your ability to instinctually 'feel' people out. Are you ready to rise above the levels of an initiate in analytical thinking? Then let's begin!

Chapter 3 – READ 'EM, SENSE EMOTIONAL ENERGY, TRUST YOUR INSTINCT

How Do I Start Reading People?

The first thing you must do is let go of your personal prejudices and adopt a holistic point of view. Here again, a famous Bruce Lee quote applies - "Adapt what is useful, reject what is useless, and add what is specifically your own." This means that you have to adapt to the parts of a person's personality that you cannot figure out naturally. They may not fall completely into any general category, but they will most likely have an affinity with some aspect of a category.

Let's look at an example of this. Suppose you meet a guy at a party. He seems attractive and kind. You think he might be interested in you. Before you decide that he is, in fact, a kind person, look at how he treats other people, especially other girls. If he pays a lot of attention to you, is gentle with his words and is giving off the right vibe, then he just might be what you want. But if he is dismissive or disparaging of other girls, then he is most likely faking his interest in you and you should steer clear of him.

Here's another example from a different perspective. Suppose you are introduced to a new colleague at work. They seem capable and organized at first glance. Their smile is charming and looks genuine. Their dedication to their work also seems legit. Here, you need to look for any signs that they might be faking it. There is a chance that everything is fine and you might be a bit paranoid. But as the brilliant writer William S. Burroughs says, "Sometimes paranoia is just having all the facts." Victory loves preparation and there is nothing wrong with analyzing someone to know their flaws. After all, everyone, including you, has at least a few.

Now that you have the basics down, let us look at something a bit more advanced. The following is a list of some of the most important things to look out for when reading people:

1. **The Approach**

    The approach is the most important thing whether you are approaching or being approached. Read the signs that they give off. Do they smile at you as they approach you? Or is it a nonchalant look? How does that handshake feel? Is it tight and firm, indicating confidence? Or is it too tight, indicating dominance? Maybe the handshake is casual, indicating indifference or even unconcern. Always bear in mind the situation and setting of the moment. Are you at work or at a party? Are you wearing something seductive or conservative? What are the signals that you may be giving off to others?

Chapter 3 – READ 'EM, SENSE EMOTIONAL ENERGY, TRUST YOUR INSTINCT

2. The Conversation

This is the point at which you truly get to gauge a person and their emotions. At the same time, this is also where you get to show your own personality. When making conversation, here are some things to consider. Do they do most of the talking or do you? What is the tone that each has adopted? Does it feel natural or put on? What are your instincts telling you?

In this scenario, you have to decide how you are going to portray yourself. Consider whether you are interested in the person and whether they are giving you enough time to frame your own thoughts and express them. Moreover, do you like the way the conversation is going?

3. The Parting

This is the final act of the play and major signals are given off here. All that was left unsaid in the conversation is going to be manifested at the ending. Mostly, the parting is going to be guided by how the preceding segments of the interaction went. If you like the person, then let them know with a smile or a touch. If you don't, then just let it slide. If the conversation carries professional obligations, then act that way and you will receive a similar response. Whenever possible, it is best to end all interactions on a positive note.

4. The Afterthought

Have you ever felt one way about an event at the time, but then felt differently afterward? That is a common feeling. Does that explain why you never get around to calling that guy or girl you met? It very well might. In any case, you should always give every interaction you have a given amount of afterthought. No need to dwell on it. Just go over it and analyze your behavior as well as that of the other person.

This reevaluation is part of the analytical process which should ideally be undertaken when you are about to go off to sleep. When done right, it can reinforce your previous judgments, give vital insights and enhance your analytical ability in the long run.

So, now we know how to break any interaction down and assess the parts individually. What more do we need to know? A lot more actually. One of the most important parts of the reading process, your instinct, still remains to be discussed. Here it is.

Chapter 3 – READ 'EM, SENSE EMOTIONAL ENERGY, TRUST YOUR INSTINCT

How Do I Use My Instinct to Analyze People?

Remember the time when you were a toddler, and your parents had an argument or there was something off in the family, you could sense it without knowing? How about that time when that guy offered you and your friend a ride back home? Didn't your instinct jump up, tell you to decline and walk right away? These are the workings of your instinct. It is the inheritance you have received from tens of thousands of years of evolution. Right from the time of our ancestors to the present day, our instinct is what has helped our species survive and evolve. It is a voice that cannot and should not be ignored. But the question becomes "How do I use my instinct actively to assess people?" Here are the answers you need:

1. **Start With the Basics**

    Just like winning is a habit, analysis is also one that you should include in your daily mental workings. Remember what you read about reading body language and behavior in the previous chapter? Make a mental checklist of all the things you think are relevant and start putting it to use.

    As you get better at analysis, you will add or subtract from that list and customize it to suit your needs. Given enough time, that list will become an integral part of your mind's inner workings. You will eventually not need to do it deliberately and your instinct will simply adapt to the new paradigm.

2. Constance

The most accomplished experts in their field will tell you that if you want to be good at something, eat, sleep and breathe it. The same goes with analyzing people. Your ability to gauge a person totally depends on how regularly you practice it. Just like regular workouts at the gym keep your body active and healthy, exercising your mental and analytical faculties has the same effect on your mind.

Make a habit of analyzing people and situations on a regular basis. Once you start, you are likely to find that you used to do a lot of analyzing instinctively anyway. The conscious effort will simply reinforce your analytical ability and make it much more refined. However, you should also be careful not to overanalyze and get trapped in a particular way of thinking. That will only stifle your ability to evolve mentally and make you a one-dimensional thinker.

Chapter 3 – READ 'EM, SENSE EMOTIONAL ENERGY, TRUST YOUR INSTINCT

3. Variety

Variety is the spice of life and it is also the perfect fodder for developing your analytical ability. Do you sometimes find yourself wishing you were in a different situation than you are in right now? What if things were to go bad all of a sudden? Would you be able to react appropriately or just fall apart?

In order to find out, you need to put yourself mentally through a variety of situations. Ask yourself how you would respond to them. If you have a particularly dire situation in mind, analyze your own response based on previous experience. The key here is to always remain grounded and realistic.

4. Empathy

This is a tricky one. Empathy is probably one of the most important emotions that we as humans have. Unfortunately, it is a double-edged sword. When you begin empathizing with other people, you might be able to understand exactly what they are feeling. However, if you empathize too much, then you are in danger of drifting off along with your trail of emotions. That is a situation you must avoid at all costs. Even if it's someone close to you that you are empathizing with, you need to maintain the proper distance between your own and their emotions. Would it help if both of you broke down during a crisis? It certainly would not.

Empathy can be a wonderful tool for instinctive analysis of others. The point is to make yourself vulnerable enough to feel other people's pain. This will let you walk in their shoes to a degree and give you some insight into what they might be feeling. If you measure this insight against your own perceived reaction, then you will see the difference. Then you will have a greater understanding of that person, your own self as well as any range of personalities that fall in between.

5. **Assimilation**

So, you have been at it for some time and now it is time to bring the different pieces of the puzzle together. Not just from when you started analyzing, but right from the first memory you have. How did you feel when you first kissed that girl? What impact did your parent's divorce have on you? Did you feel like you have achieved something when you got the promotion? Ask yourself these questions and then assimilate whatever answers you get to reconstructing or evolving your personality.

Chapter 3 – READ 'EM, SENSE EMOTIONAL ENERGY, TRUST YOUR INSTINCT

Let your instinct be the decider on what is important and what is not, and then take the best and forge yourself a new way of thinking, living and being.

6. Reductionism – Simply Simplify

For those of you who might have read or come in contact with the field of philosophy, reductionism might not be a new concept. However, for the sake of refreshment and simple explanation, it bears repeating. In the most basic of terms, reductionism is reducing any given system into smaller parts. This makes them easy to understand individually as well as when taken together.

So for example, if you see a tragic situation, like a death in the family, then two different people might have two different reactions. The father might become stoic and accept it, but the mother might be hysterical and distraught. Despite these two wildly different reactions, the core value remains the same – loss.

Now, when it comes to analyzing people, once you have done it for long enough and assimilated all your knowledge, it is time to simplify. This will make the system more effective and easy to implement. Take two differing reactions and try to find where they overlap.

Most often you will find that your instinct already knows the answer, it is just a matter of reaching it consciously.

7. Occam's Razor

If you understood the principle of reductionism, you will have no trouble understanding this at all. Have you ever wondered when two competing ideas are presented to you, which one should be chosen? Occam's razor is the answer. This simple problem-solving method says that when all things are equal, the shortest path is the best one.

In other words, it could be that Ryan really feels it is necessary for all members of his team to work as a unit and therefore, goes out of his way to ensure their compliance. But the idea that Ryan simply likes to dominate others might be even truer. Similarly, Jane might just be a really caring mother who loves her children a whole lot. Or she might be compensating for the parental love she never got by giving it to her children.

So, it is easy to see how this principle might solve a lot of analytical problems. Trust your instinct to tell you which one you should go for and the one you choose will most

Chapter 3 – READ 'EM, SENSE EMOTIONAL ENERGY, TRUST YOUR INSTINCT

likely be the shorter, simpler explanation. Be warned however that oversimplification can result in you missing out on vital details that should not be overlooked to get a true picture of anyone's personality.

8. The Path Ahead

So, now you have done almost everything you need to develop your instinctual analytical ability. What comes next? Well, that is up to you. It is your own system, so adding and subtracting from it is your own personal choice. Ideally, whenever you come across an analytical problem, you should try to fit it into your system. If it doesn't fit in, then you may need to adjust your thinking pattern and develop a more sophisticated system.

Remember that life does not need to make sense all the time. Coincidence is never a good explanation, but it is sometimes the only one we have. Again, you should trust your gut to tell you where you should go and how you should approach new situations. Be open to change and a path will be revealed sooner than later.

Keeping all these things in mind, you can start your own analytical system. There is no problem in borrowing from other sources and adding to your ideas. In fact, that is the core idea being empathic – feeling from another person's point of view, bringing the range of emotions you felt, simplifying them and adding them to your own comprehension of human sentiment.

Change is constant and what is not changing is already dead. Do you not feel a bit constricted when your personal relationships don't give you room to grow? How about when you see your professional career slowing down? Does it not feel like it is time for a change to reignite the flames of your ambition? The same goes for every experience you have in life. Your analytical ability rests on practice and perseverance. Expose yourself to as much variety as you can take and you are sure to mature your ability in quick time.

Whenever you are feeling like you have strayed from the path, go back to the basics. Figure out the who, what, when, where, and why, and build on that. If you keep things simple, then chances are you are going to be able to hit the mark more often than not.

As stated at the beginning of the chapter, this is intermediate level stuff. Before you proceed to the next chapter, it is highly advised that you go over each and every detail of this chapter thoroughly. Only then you will be able to benefit from the next chapter where we are going to look at different personality types from a psychological point of view.

Chapter 3 – READ 'EM, SENSE EMOTIONAL ENERGY, TRUST YOUR INSTINCT

Are you ready to become a master analyzer? Then keep reading!

CHAPTER 4 - UNDERSTANDING HUMAN PERSONALITY TYPES - DISC MODEL of HUMAN BEHAVIOR

Always be yourself, express yourself, have faith in yourself, do not go out and look for a successful personality and duplicate it.

---------- *Bruce Lee, Actor and Martial Artist*

Did it ever occur to you that some people have very similar personality types? Particularly, their personality traits seem to match quite a lot. If you have then you might actually be onto something significant.

Just as is the case with our genes, our personalities also share a lot of commonalities. For example, two people working in an office might have the same goal/task-oriented outlook while also having a people-friendly aspect to their personality. Similarly, two siblings living in a home with their parents might share the same kind of love for video games.

Despite the similarities in our nature, there is no denying that there are also many subtle yet significant differences. Studying them and understanding where personalities overlap and where they strike out their own path can be a healthy way to go about dissecting the human approach to life.

This chapter is going to go into full-on psychology. It is going to examine one of the most popular models for human personalities called the DISC model. This acronym stands for Dominant, Inspiring, Supportive and Cautious.

Yes, there are many models for understanding human personality types but most of those adopt a negativist approach to understanding human personalities. If you have some experience in dealing with people, you might agree that having a positive approach to human personality is the best way forward.

Are you ready to understand the inner workings of people's minds according to their personality types? Then, let's start.

But first, a little background.

Origins of the DISC model

The beginnings of human personality modeling can be traced as far back as the time of the Greeks. Hippocrates in particular had

CHAPTER 4 - UNDERSTANDING HUMAN PERSONALITY TYPES - DISC MODEL of HUMAN BEHAVIOR

a rather advanced model of understanding personalities based on their inherent traits.

Why do we come back time and again to these figures and ideas? The reason is that people from those times had a very different view of life. Nonetheless, the simplicity of their existence prompted them to question things much more rigorously and religiously than modern-day common people.

Also, the fact that these people basically laid the foundations for what was to become the human quest for self-understanding is important. Without them, we would still be trying to formulate the fundamentals which we now naturally assume to be true.

Building on the groundwork laid down by the Greek tradition, Dr. William Marston published a book in 1928 called The Emotions of Normal People. This book laid the foundations for the development of the DISC model.

Now, that you know the background of this model, let us begin with understanding the fundamentals of personality types.

The Fundamentals of the DISC Model

Have you ever wondered why some people are more capable than others in the social sense? Did it ever cross your mind that even if you don't have their inborn gift for social competence, you can still develop the quality? Understanding the DISC model may hold the key to all the answers you have always wanted to find out about yourself and others.

Let's begin by reducing people's personality types to four broad categories - Outgoing & Reserved and Task-oriented & People-oriented. Most people have two of characteristics from each of these polar opposite traits.

Be aware that this does not mean that some people do not have three traits at the same time. Sometimes people can have all four traits at the same time but only two may be apparent in any given situation. So, even though this model is going to give you a holistic idea of how to read people, you should not be too quick judge and rather let time unfold the layers of personalities on your subjects.

Outgoing Personalities

Now, let us look at the inherent traits which are common to all four of these abovementioned characteristics. Outgoing people are naturally more socially capable. They are easy to be friends with and can form social bonds very easily. These people are often found working in jobs that deal a lot with people. One

CHAPTER 4 - UNDERSTANDING HUMAN PERSONALITY TYPES - DISC MODEL of HUMAN BEHAVIOR

example of such a job would be working as an HR manager in a corporate enterprise.

Reserved Personalities

Reserved people, in contrast, are shyer in their interactions with people and make friends very cautiously. However, when they have let a particular person into their inner circle, they tend to be very loyal towards them. Most reserved people tend to flourish in jobs that deal with numbers or stats than actual people. Examples of this kind of job are economists, financial analysts or librarians.

People-Oriented Personalities

As their title suggests, people-oriented individuals are very capable of interacting with and handling others. They have a very wide social palette and are mostly able to interact and negotiate with all kinds of people. A people-oriented worker is a great asset to have in a professional setting. They will most likely be adept at handling a team of people. Depending upon their years of experience, you can also be certain that they would excel at all jobs that require handling people tactfully, whether that is PR or HR.

Task-Oriented Personalities

Task-oriented people are like machines. They keep digging away at the work, sometimes even to the detriment of their health. You know workaholics right? That's a task-oriented person. For such people, whether they are at home or at work or anywhere else, the task at hand is the most important thing. These people can make some of the best subordinates in your enterprise. They are dedicated to their work and like to have their actions do the talking for them. They also work well with other people as long as the team stays true to the task. Since task-oriented personalities work with such dedication, you can find them in almost any line of work. They are also very likely to be successful thanks to their unflinching tenacity and work ethic.

So now we understand what the most basic kinds of personality types are. The question now becomes how do you spot them? Here's how you should go about doing that:

Things to Remember Before you Begin Defining Personality Traits

The first thing to do when identifying personality traits is to observe carefully. Now, this might seem very obvious but it is not. Most people don't even understand the difference between

CHAPTER 4 - UNDERSTANDING HUMAN PERSONALITY TYPES - DISC MODEL of HUMAN BEHAVIOR

seeing, looking and observing. In order to be a capable people analyzer, you are going to need to do all three at the same time.

In other words, you are going to have to look like you are seeing, observe what you are looking at and see what you observe. Let's break all three of these actions down (reductionism!). When you see something, you just happen to roll your vision over certain objects that caught your attention. When you look, you are deliberately trying to see something. The difference between seeing and looking is that the first one is casual and involuntary while the second is serious and voluntary.

Now, when you observe, you look and see at the same time. It is very important for you to not stare or glare at the subject of your observation to ensure you don't make them uncomfortable or self-conscious. That is why you should 'observe like you are seeing.' This might seem a bit tricky at first, but once you understand the underlying significance, you will most certainly be able to appreciate the difference.

The next step is to identify their personality traits. Once you have your observation game going strong, you need to start considering what you are going to observe. Should I pay attention to what they are wearing? Or should I start with the way they walk and move? Should my observation be on the outward or the inward? These are some of the many questions you have to consider. However, it is also important to understand that STARTING is essential.

Don't get bogged down by methodology. You don't need to follow a strict pattern. You should improvise when reading personalities to see how they fit the four basic types.

Now, let's move on to understanding how the DISC model further categorizes personalities based on traits.

Defining Personality Traits

According to the DISC model, different personalities exhibit different kinds of drives and inclinations. For the sake of clarity, they will be discussed here so you can pinpoint which personality types you find most often on the subject of your observation.

Remember that this is only a theoretical model and the people you actually meet in real life may or may not conform exactly to these typesets. It is your job to identify their most dominant personality traits and see where they overlap with other personality traits.

Take the following explanations as a benchmark for yourself to build on. As said in the previous chapters, remember to customize your system to suit your needs and interpretations.

CHAPTER 4 - UNDERSTANDING HUMAN PERSONALITY TYPES - DISC MODEL of HUMAN BEHAVIOR

Don't be afraid of breaking down a system and reconstructing it if this gives you a better understanding of human personalities.

With that said, let us dive into the four major personalities according to the DISC model.

D – Dominant, Driving, Doer

These people are the most extroverted kind that you can find anywhere. They are easy to talk to and usually pursue a very overt agenda. In the domestic arena, D personalities can be really good partners who can lead by example and foster the same driven personality in their children. In the work domain, D personalities are seen as leaders who have a lot of ambition and are naturally predisposed towards taking charge of things.

Have you ever met someone who resembles this description? If yes, then it might be worthwhile to study them. If you want to develop these qualities in yourself, then studying someone who exhibits them becomes even more important. D personalities are easily noticeable because they are so outgoing. They love to lead and take charge of situations. When there is trouble, you can almost always be sure that such personalities are going to act reliably.

On the flipside, however, D personalities are also somewhat elitist in nature. This means that they will mostly only associate with people who are driven like themselves. They also don't normally have it in them to inspire people as much as the next personality on our list. However, they can harness the potential of each person and serve as very effective leaders in all forms of governance and administration.

I – Inspiring, Interactive, Interesting

I personalities have an inborn talent for inspiring themselves and others. Many dreamers and ambitious individuals fall into this category. If you were to go through some of the most charismatic leaders in world history, you will find that many of them were a healthy combination of I and D-type personalities. Since these kinds of people are so full of hope and goals, it is easy for them to influence people with their enthusiasm.

That is why in the domestic ambit, I personalities are exceptionally good partners. They not only inspire their spouses to be their best but also prompt their children to do the same. Professionally speaking, I personalities can be very optimistic ideators or conceptualizers. They can work marvelously with ideas and refine them to achieve short and long-term business goals.

Does this sound like someone you know? If so, then you should take a closer look at how they behave. Chances are that these I

CHAPTER 4 - UNDERSTANDING HUMAN PERSONALITY TYPES - DISC MODEL of HUMAN BEHAVIOR

personalities will not only showcase their raw enthusiasm for you in stark terms but also infect you with some of their zeal.

Be wary, however. There is a huge chasm between an idea and the ground reality that exists. It can very easily be that the ideas that such personalities come up with are not feasible. In this case, they are very prone to be discouraged and even depressed. Also, it is possible that such personalities may completely and utterly disregard your opposing point of view.

If you want to be friends with such a personality, it is best to bask in the aura of their positivity but also stay grounded enough to know realities. Dreaming is important. But without doing, it has no value.

S – Supportive, Steady, Stable

S personalities are probably the most reliable of the lot. They are caring, kind and considerate. They also like to remain on the safe side, which is rarely a bad thing. These kinds of people are best at supporting others and enabling them to rise to higher heights. However, since they are conventionally seen as subservient, they can often be neglected or left behind by other more aggressive or enterprising personality types.

Do you have any such person in your life? If so, then you should be careful as not to disregard them. S personality types are some of the best and most long-term friends that you can have. When D personalities will abandon you for not being able to keep up with them, and I personalities do the same because you are not as energized as they are, it will be S personality people who will be your bedrock. They will help and support you and enable you to weather any storm.

Do you know that saying 'Girls date bad guys and marry the good guys?' That is a rather accurate description of the different kinds of personality types you are likely to encounter in your life. If you have an S personality person as a spouse, you probably already know how valuable they are. These people are amazing with children and can bond very deeply with their kids over even the most commonplace of things.

On the other hand, being safe and stable also means that they do not have the potential for making great leaps. So, while dating a D or I personality might be fun and exciting, an S personality will not be able to match up in that department. What you will get from them is stability and reliability, which is the cornerstone of your personal life. Even professionally, S personalities are reliable workers and you can trust them to get the job done. They might not have the tools for rapid innovation or game-changing ideas, but they do have the consistency to chart continuous growth.

CHAPTER 4 - UNDERSTANDING HUMAN PERSONALITY TYPES - DISC MODEL of HUMAN BEHAVIOR

C – Cautious, Competent, Careful

C personalities are highly regarded for their careful nature. They are best at being guarded and conservative. This might not make them very attractive at first, but to someone who has life experience, being careful is a very valuable asset. As the old saying goes 'slow and steady wins the race' so goes how C personalities approach life and living.

If you have ever come across such a personality, then you probably know that these people were not willing to open up easily. But you should not be disheartened if they do not respond with the same amount of enthusiasm as you. They have their own style of working and if you give it time then they will eventually warm up to you.

Let's look at these kinds of personalities with an analogy. There are two investors in the market – A and B. A makes a lot of trades and invests in high-risk stocks. As a result, they stand a chance of earning a lot and also losing an equal amount. Over the long term, A's financial stability is questionable because of their investment pattern.

On the other hand, B is an exceptionally cautious investor who only invests in stocks after thoroughly vetting their previous performance. When they make the investment, they understand that even if the market value goes down, they will not suffer a big loss. However, this also means that they do not stand to gain as much as A. Nevertheless, over the long run, B stands to receive much more profit than A.

The same goes for C personalities. While they might be picky and choosy about who they open up to and let into their world, they are also a wonder to have in your life as friends and partners. If you are someone who likes to stay on the wild side, then a C personality individual can be a literal boon for you. If you listen to their advice, then it is quite possible that you will avoid making regrettable mistakes.

Some Further Tips

Now you have a fair idea of what to expect from each personality type. Always remember that situation and setting are the most important things when doing an analysis. What is the context? What is the reference? What background is the person coming from? These questions are inherent to your understanding of different types of personalities.

Again, customize your system to develop your own. The DISC model is a general guide which can help you identify and track different personality traits and their development over time. Do you think that none of the DISC types are defining a person?

CHAPTER 4 - UNDERSTANDING HUMAN PERSONALITY TYPES - DISC MODEL of HUMAN BEHAVIOR

Then just create a new type. You can also define a personality based on the range of emotions they express or the kind of 'aura' they carry.

However, you must always act on evidence. Pseudoscientific theories can be very attractive, but without actual evidence to back them up, they are just theories. Never fall for the misconceived notion that just because you can figure a person out, you will be able to guess everything they think or are capable of. With enough forethought and experience, you too will be able to become a master analyzer with everyone's personality at your fingertips.

In the next chapter, we are going to talk about the practicalities of people analysis. We will discuss how to turn theory into systems and get the best out of every conversation. Are you ready to take your theories and test them in the acid bath of reality? Then read on!

CHAPTER 5 – GETTING the BEST OUT of EVERY CONVERSATION

"I believe that words are strong, that they can overwhelm what we fear when fear seems more awful than life is good."

----------- Andrew Solomon, Author

Conversations are the key to understanding a person completely. While you might be able to analyze someone based on how they walk or talk with others, your clearest picture will be formed once you have a personal conversation with them.

Has it ever happened that when you came across someone, you formed a mental picture about them which was completely different from the impression you got when you spoke to them? It happens to even the most capable and experienced analyzers. The reason behind this is that people only see two things about another person – what that person wants to show you and what you want to see.

Virtually all observation is colored by prejudice. It is your job as an observer to become as objective as possible. If you don't, then you are very likely to fall into one single train of thought and define people accordingly. This will lead to mistaken, biased ideas and observations.

Keeping this in mind, let us look at how conversations guide and shape our observations, and how they correct or alter our preformed notions. We will also look at how you can get the best out of every conversation and turn even seemingly inimical interactions in your favor.

So, assimilate all that you have learned through the course of the book, reduce it to a simple, direct system and use Occam's Razor to arrive at conclusions quickly and efficiently. Are you ready for becoming a truly masterful analyzer? Then, let's dive in!

Question Everything

Questioning what you see, hear and gather from your senses is at the heart of your knowledge acquisition. If you do not question the nature of things and the reasons behind their occurrence, you will only see what is apparent about them at the surface. Only by going deeper than the skin can you truly find out about their true nature.

CHAPTER 5 – GETTING the BEST OUT of EVERY CONVERSATION

The first thing you must do is question everything. This doesn't mean that you oppose and resist everything. Rather, flow with their current, be involved and yet stay detached enough to see the larger picture.

For example, do you understand why your spouse is so keen on sending the kids away to summer camp? Do they really want the children to utilize their time in the best possible way or do they want to give you some alone-time? Could it be both?

Similarly, have you been wondering what the reason behind the budgetary reallocations at work is? Is it based on the individual performances of departments? Or is it a consequence of policy change? What do you think motivated the top dogs to come to this decision?

In these two scenarios, it becomes necessary to 'feel' out the truth hidden behind and act appropriately. And what is the best way to do that? A deep and thorough analysis!

Mid-Conversation Analysis

Let's be very clear about this. When you are in the middle of a conversation, you will not have the time to do a deliberate analysis. If you keep thinking about why something is happening, you are likely to lose the flow of the conversation.

That is why you must not analyze deliberately when in the middle of a conversation. Rather, it should be a background app running on your mental operating system. This ability will take some time to develop. It will only come to you once you have already developed a fair bit of analytical acumen and can do it instinctively.

As always, let your instinct be the guide towards impromptu analysis. This will save you the trouble of devoting your mental faculties towards analysis during conversations but will still give you enough fodder to act appropriately. In the simplest of senses, when body, mind, and spirit are in tune with one another, it is possible to be on the button.

Let's now look at some very handy tips for developing analytical abilities that can be used on the fly. Remember that your analytical ability is dependent on how much you practice it. If you make a habit of analyzing people and situations, then you are far more likely to be successful in the instinctual analysis.

Developing Analytical Ability for In-Conversation Analysis

Does it ever occur to you that the before and after of any conversation is actually more important than the conversation

CHAPTER 5 – GETTING the BEST OUT of EVERY CONVERSATION

itself? If you have thought along these lines, then you might have actually struck gold.

Just like the climax of a movie, it is the buildup to a conversation that gives it its value and potency. For example, when you meet a long-time friend of yours after a long time, you are very likely to have a more stimulating conversation than if you met them regularly.

Similarly, when the company contract is finally signed, it might be a momentous occasion. But it is the buildup up to the signing which gives it the importance it enjoys. Without the buildup, there would be little value in anything.

Let's take a look at this from a different point of view. Suppose one of your friends is a rather rash driver. They have a string of speeding tickets but don't seem to show any signs of addressing this problem. When you hear that they had an accident, it might be distressing, but in reality, you probably saw it coming.

Just as with situations in life, the buildup to conversations is all-important. If you know that the boss wants to have a word with you, then you will naturally feel nervous, excited or curious about it and grant credence to this future conversation.

With that in mind, let's examine some of the ways you can grasp the 'feel' of any conversation and conduct a situational analysis:

HOW TO ANALYZE PEOPLE

1. Understand the Undercurrent

The undercurrent is a sentiment that is running opposite to the vibe of the situation.

For example, if you are visiting a car lot and the salesperson is pitching you a sales line that they don't seem to be enthused about, then it is quite likely that they themselves do not believe in the product they are endorsing. You should then probably consider buying a different car.

Similarly, if your spouse is verbally supportive of your mother-in-law visiting but actually seems to be put off, then chances are they don't particularly relish the idea.

The undercurrent is an important indicator of the truth of the given conversation. If you can notice it, then you might be able to guess the actual facts behind the matter rather than taking the conversation at face value.

So, when in the middle of a conversation, cultivate the habit of picking up on the undercurrent. Remember the body language indicators discussed in earlier chapters? These are signs of undercurrents that you can incorporate into your instinctual analytical ability.

CHAPTER 5 – GETTING the BEST OUT of EVERY CONVERSATION

2. Spot the Overtones

Overtones are the implications made by a conversation. They are suggestions and indicators to what the person wants you to think and believe.

Here's an example of an overtone. If you are on a date and the person keeps referring to their bad relationships in the past, then the conversation has overtones of trust issues. If you want to act on the suggestion they are making, then you should make them feel that you are trustworthy. This will let them open up to you and share their inner thoughts and feelings more freely.

Let's look at the previous salesperson example. If the salesperson endorsing the car you are looking at seems to be highly energetic and is frequently citing the many reasons why it is a great ride for you and your family, then the conversation carries a strong sales-oriented overtone. It will be up to you to decide how you want to take that overtone and make your purchase decision.

Overtones can be great for understanding the intent behind what a person says. They can reveal the true intent behind the conversation and give you an edge over the person you are speaking to. The main difference between the undercurrent and the overtone is that the former is involuntary while the latter is voluntary. Knowing which applies where is a sure way of figuring out the true intent behind a conversation.

3. Motives are Mandatory

When starting a conversation, every person has a particular motive behind it. If you are at work and a colleague is telling you how to do your task better, then their motive might be to help you out. On the other hand, it could also mean that they are hoping you do a bad job and get reprimanded by the boss.

How you gauge a person's motive is largely dependent on your own thinking process and the observations you have made before. It is unhelpful to be naïve but it is also unhelpful to be overly clever. Accurately understanding the motives behind any conversation requires a balanced approach.

In the example mentioned above, whether the colleague is helping you out or plotting your downfall will largely depend on their previous behavior. As always, the buildup is most important. This will indicate the true motives behind the words and actions of your colleague.

CHAPTER 5 – GETTING the BEST OUT of EVERY CONVERSATION

If you observe people carefully and give yourself some time, then you will most likely be able to spot the motives behind any person's words and actions. Train your instinct to spot the motives of every individual you meet, and you are sure to develop a robust analytical ability.

4. Instincts and Impulses

Most people are not as cerebral as they should be. They are led by their emotions and find satisfaction in fulfilling their natural impulses and drives. While it is important to let your instinct be the guide, it is also important to question your instinct and impulses. You can also do this for other people.

For example, do you really think Ashley's decision to break up with her boyfriend because he got fired is right? Is it ethically correct or more importantly, can you endorse this decision as something you would do too? How about Bob's choice to cut ties with his business partner when he found out he is engaging in insider trading? Do you agree with his decision?

Depending upon your internal moral compass, you will come to a decision about how you feel about other people's decisions. Sometimes you might have to act tactfully. So, while you might not agree with your boss firing your colleague because they messed up a project, it would be wise to keep your opinion to yourself.

There is no substitute for common sense. Thankfully it can be cultivated. You have to keep your interests and instincts in line in order to make the most of them. Learn to spot the instincts and impulses of other people and gauge how likely they are to be led by them. By doing so, you will have a big picture view of their personality and how you should act in a conversation.

Now you have a fair idea of the four major forces you must learn to spot in any conversation. If you religiously develop the habit of spotting these, it is very likely that you will be able to master the art of analyzing people with a decent amount of accuracy.

However, an important thing to remember is that just as doing no analysis is a problem, doing excessive analysis is also a problem. As with all things in life, there should be a healthy balance. Sometimes, it is best to go with your gut and act on impulse. These are situations when you are relaxing with your friends or partners.

At other times, it is indeed important to be highly analytical and retain a professional frame of mind. Situations in which you are

CHAPTER 5 – GETTING the BEST OUT of EVERY CONVERSATION

financially invested or have professional obligations, are good examples of such scenarios. The best frame of mind to be in is being calm while also being analytical...

With that said, let us now look at how you can stop yourself from overanalyzing conversations and situations. These tips will save you from headaches and heartaches in the long run.

How Not to Overanalyze

People who are very good at analyzing others often get the mistaken notion inside their minds that analysis is required at every turn. While it is almost always good to gauge the drop before you take the plunge, sometimes it is best to go with the flow and act on impulse. This can lead to great stimulation and even bonding with other people. Overanalyzing can be a literal stab through the heart of all the fun you can have. So, here are some tips to prevent yourself from analyzing too much:

1. **Stop Overthinking** – Intelligent people often tire themselves out by overthinking. You must maintain a balance between thinking and feeling. Only then can you truly be one in body, mind, and spirit. Overthinking is as poisonous to your mental health as lack of thinking. It is best to devote enough time to your thinking process without exceeding your normal limit. If you would like to

be able to think more, then develop the ability slowly instead of overexerting your mind. Just like weight training for the body, the mind can be trained to handle a heavy load as well.

2. **Don't be Judgmental** – People are judgmental because they feel threatened by others in some way. You should develop your personality so that even if you find that someone has an ability or possession that you would like, it doesn't make you feel inadequate. Even if there is some sentiment leading to a negative image of yourself or the other person, you should preferably try to mold it so that you can evolve through it rather than be restricted by it.

3. **Don't be Prejudiced** – Being prejudiced is just about the worst thing you can do for your analytical ability. Even if you have years of experience in dealing with people, you should always treat each person individually. This way, you will be able to gauge their ability without being sidetracked by preconceived notions. Having an open mind that is receptive to changes is instrumental to an effective system. This is the reason why generation gaps exist. To overcome this, you must be understanding and tolerant of new ways of thinking.

CHAPTER 5 – GETTING the BEST OUT of EVERY CONVERSATION

4. **Engage in Constructive Criticism and Comparison** –Comparison can be a great way to understand similarities and differences. However, never engage in negative comparison because it does not help. Always try to be positive and focus on what can be done to improve things. Negative criticism makes you a negative person and no one likes to be associated with someone who can only point out flaws without showing how to overcome them.

5. **Be Situational** – Perhaps the biggest mistake people make while analyzing others is taking their analysis out of context. This can lead to many faulty assumptions. In order to get an accurate read on someone, you must read the situation first. What is the situation and setting? That is the fundamental question to ask yourself and based on this, your next line of inquiry should follow.

Whenever you are in doubt if you have gone on the right analytical path or not, remember to reduce things down to the simplest terms. However, be careful not to become simplistic, which means that you reduce things so much that they lose their essence.

In other words, always keep the core emotion or value of any idea intact when scaling it down. For example, grief can be reduced to loss but not to frustration. Similarly, elation can be reduced to joy but not ignorance.

With this, we come to the conclusion of the chapter. It is highly recommended that you read and reread every aspect of this chapter until you have them fit perfectly into your analytical system. Don't be hungry for insight. Let it come to you naturally and you will surely develop a great analytical ability.

CONCLUSION

Analysis, when done right, can be a great way to boost your potential and the potential of those around you. This book has focused on covering all aspects of analyzing people with the most practical situations in mind.

Through the theoretical patterns explained in this book, you are sure to develop your analytical ability. The key is to remain basic while also evolving the ability to understand and adapt to new personality paradigms and situations.

Remember that any good system is in constant evolution and if you rigorously follow this advice, then you are very likely to find your own system constantly adapting to new things you encounter in life. This will not just ensure that your analytical ability is relevant to your unique style and needs but is also supportive of those around you.

Also keep in mind that positivity is the best policy when it comes to analyzing people. In order help yourself and others around you grow into better human beings, you should always be optimistic and look for ways to enhance potential and not throttle it.

As the great American writer Ernst Hemingway said, "The world is a fine place and worth fighting for." Taking a cue from his words, you should use your analytical ability for the good of as many people as possible.

Happy Analyzing!

www.ingramcontent.com/pod-product-compliance
Lightning Source LLC
Chambersburg PA
CBHW070203230526
45471CB00002B/803